Empty

Laura Benbenaissa

BookLeaf
Publishing

India | USA | UK

Presentation by *BookLeaf Publishing*

Web: www.bookleafpub.com

E-mail: info@bookleafpub.com

ISBN: 9789358310078

First edition 2023

DEDICATION

To Rachid, my first love, & to Sophia and Julia
for loving their mommy beyond words.

ACKNOWLEDGEMENT

I would like to express my appreciation for my encounters in life. I begin my expression with the little family I have created. To my first love, who has shown me the world and to my daughters in which I endured chaos and learned patience. Many thanks to my family who had to put up with my stubbornness and attitude. Lastly, to my true friends who have always been by my side, who gave me confidence and the ability to be myself. Much love to you all.

PREFACE

Writing is often a tool used to escape a certain mindset. It allows others to leave behind these temporary thoughts. For most, it is an escape from the fears and hopes that swallow you whole. It becomes a place of learning. These poems allowed me to express myself during the darkest of times, where I hurt the most and my tears refuse to stop. Hopefully I have helped you, the reader, to express yourself with the power of writing.

Why?

Why me?
Why hate?
Why soothing tea that does not soothe?
Why checkmate?
Why conspire?
Why desire?
Why a heart that cannot prove?
Why inquire?
Why seethe?
Why beneath?
Why do I feel so uncovered?
Why leave?
Why Me........

Blue

An unspeakable notion once brought to mind
simplicity of blue and treasures to find.
This color relaxes and offers such peace
its wonder and amazement never to cease.
Blue is an emotion, like sadness and joy
a child that's pleased with a brand new toy.
This beauty varies on the color spectrum,
some names too creative not to accept them.
From teal to iris, cyan, and periwinkle
in the midnight sky where the stars all twinkle.
Cornflower and cobalt and aquamarine
indigo and lapis and others unseen.
The cerulean kind of October sky
Hawaiian turquoise waves come crashing so
high!
The feelings that blue creates helps me to feel
like nothing could hurt me, only help me to heal.
Each color shows power in names that it uses
taking months to heal from internal bruises.
The various shades of blue help disguise
all the tears that I cry from my hazel eyes.
The hurt that I feel I cannot tell today
but I'm sure that the blues will all go away.

Daughters

Sugar and spice and everything nice, what girls
are meant to be.
What you don't know, I will show, unlocking the
door with a key.
Sweet as honey, love is pure, what you'd want in
a wife,
low and behold, the darkness comes, watch out
for the hidden knife.
My girls I've taught them everything, and always
to be strong.
Don't make them mad, you will regret, making
them do wrong.
They stand up tall, you think them weak, assume
they're circumspect.
Better watch out, revenge they seek, don't show
them disrespect!
Sugar and spice and everything nice, and just a
little sass.
To them be true, or what they'll do, is kick you
in the ass

Crazy

I tried so hard, can't let you see
locked the door, threw away the key
pushed you away, then tried to hide
thousands of thoughts, racing through my mind
hidden from view, a demon stands by
making me say things, making me lie
forced to say words, I do not mean
hurting you so, my tears unseen
satisfied for now, it remains hidden
broken inside, I become bedridden
can't show you how, to understand me
my heart is burned, my soul unfree
Leave now, and go away!
can't take anymore, you can't stay
gave you more reasons, to hate me more
led the way, to the wide open door
my brain on fire, too hard to explain
what you have seen now, a person insane

Truth

Thoughts
Air
No one cares
Dreams
Lies
Compromise
Heartache
Trying
Inside crying
Love
Tears
Untold fears
Happy
Sadness
Uncontrolled Madness
Darkness
Hope
Trying to Cope
Wanting
And needing
My heart is bleeding
Hold me
It's cold
Words unfold
Truth

Near
Want you to hear
Pain
Stay
Don't go away
Trying
Chance
One last dance
Me
You
Let's continue

Not Meant to Be

At night the tears fall down
escaping from my eyes
the sound I try to drown
despite my many tries.
My heart is broke in two
and I feel all alone
I wish they only knew
what chills me to the bone.
The tears begin to slow
and sleep will soon begin
nightmares will start to grow
and a shiver across my skin.
No matter what I try
this mess I cannot fix
I give in and just sigh
and let my mind play tricks.

Colors

Roses grow wild and full of thorns
Tiger lilies open up wide
Sun is shining and the rays are warm
Grass all around soft and tempting
Ocean waves ebb and flow
Jeans are damp from the warm water
Lavender laces with the ocean breeze

Dark to Light

9

Ravens
Crows
Darkness grows
Gray
Black
Panic attack
Solace
Peace
Mind at ease
Safe
Home
Not Alone

Love Song of Misery

At night the tears fall down, hard to understand
why they must creep out, into an unknown land.
If they only knew, what chills me to the bone
what makes the blood slow down, leaving me
alone.
The cold of night creeps in, my mind it can't
escape
the thoughts begin to torment, into a bitter rape.
I am left confused, wrapped in all this fear
I have lost control, can't take the wheel and steer
Alone I'll always be, because they will never try
to help me from the dark place, where I slowly
die.

Opposites

Royals and Rebels
Black and White
Night and Day
Day and Night

Stay or go
Near and far
Smiles or tears
Oceans or stars

Late or early
Right and wrong
Hands and feet
Poem or song

His or hers
Hear and see
Me and you
You and me

elle

Living a Life of Luxury
Leggings, Lunches, Lounging
Liquor, Lucious , Louis Vutton
Lexus, Lamborghini, Limousines
Leather, Lace, Luxury yacht
Lululemon, Liquid gold, Liposuction
Looks, Lashes, Lingerie
Laughing, Loving, and Longevity

Haiku's

The moon's silvery
glow shines bright above the sea
as a warm breeze blows

A dragonfly posed
over a pond and softly
lands on a lily

A waterfall glides
over rocks to a stream where
little fishes swim

The rain falls softly
dancing on the pale beach sand
under the moonlight

Tears

Vastness
Empty
Hollow
A heart with a hole
You can see right thru, slowly breaking
Crackling
Crumbling
Torn apart
The stillness of the night, bright stars
And then it rains
Dripping
Dropping
Tears from the sky

Perfect

I will be your perfection, in the mirror your
reflection
I will be logical and sane, your words etched
into my brain
I will work hard at staying fit, nothing could
ever make me quit
I will make money and get a house, for you I'll
be the perfect spouse
I will fix my nails and hair done too, gorgeous
makeup, just for you
I will have soft skin and smell great, 1-10 what
would you rate?
I will wear the latest styles, be patient please this
may take awhile
I will love with all my heart, beautiful
beginnings from the start
But what if those things, I cannot be?
Is this the end of you and me?
I can be a mother, sister, friend, and a wife for
you until the end
I can be there when you cannot sleep, secrets I
will always keep
I can help you smile when you are sad, and keep
you calm when you are mad

I can be there when you want to travel, I cannot
let our life unravel.
I can wake in the morning and hold you dear,
sweet words I whisper in your ear
I can do better than I was before, I love our life
deep to the core
I can be perfect for you and me, because what
we are, others can't see.
I can promise this, please take this in, forever us,
a forever win.

Numb

My mind is an infinite mess. I try so hard to be happy, but one disturbed thought and everything goes dark. In the dark place I get lost. I weigh in the good and bad, the past and what my future holds. It's too hard to live in the present so I will stay in the darkness longer. Hiding from the truth. If it can't find me I'll be safe. Depression seeps in and so does the panic. My anxiety is haunting me to my core. I want to be happy but I am alone. Who do I trust? The one person that I love and trusted has left me. He became broken and fell out of love. This kind of love I will never have again. I remain unsteady, fearful of being alone. I had something great and I let it go. Selfish, stupid, and naïve. I could have had it all. Now I sit alone with sadness, feeling utterly hopeless. Tears continuously stream down my face. If only he understood the demons I fight in my head. The company they keep is poisonous and I want them gone. The more I cry the more pain I feel in my chest. It aches to wake up from this nightmare. Dreams make everything feel alright but when I open my eyes everything hurts again. If others didn't depend on me I don't know where I'd be. For now I will be lost in my infinite mind.

You and I

You took a chance with me
You stole my heart
You soothe my mind
You comfort my fears
You hold me tight
You wipe the tears
You engage my thoughts
You make me mad
You loved me
You love life
You love your family
You love yourself
You were happy
I made you mad
I made you hate
I made you leave
I made you regret
I made you lose your mind
I made you not want to be home
I made you wish you never met me
I made you crazy
I made you desperate for an out
I made you feel unimportant
I made you feel unsupported
I made you feel unloved

I made you hide
I made you say goodbye

Two Worlds

You love to travel, it's an urge and a need
While I prefer the books that I read
We both end up so far away
Ready to start a brand new day
You enjoy the sights and delicious food
While deep in the story, it captures my mood
You walk along quiet beaches, so clean
While I read a war against the queen!
The sights are glorious and fill your heart
I can't stop now, such a good part!
Your heart is full, you long to stay
I love this story, what now will they say?
There lies the problem, the distance I fear
Keeping us apart, and keeping us here
Reality wakes me and I fill with dread
Alone in the night, crawling into bed
Stories are borrowed, my life is not true
I realize too late, all I want is you
Separate worlds we now live, I caused you to go
Hurtful words were said, the distance now grows
Shocked to my core, I try to breathe
What can I do to make you believe?
Changes are made, I want you to see
I believe in fate, we were meant to be
Anything I'll do, for it's you that I want

To love and to hold, I'm over this stunt
One world we shall live, it can be done
Please try again because you are the one

Gone

Sad eyes; the reflection of a lonely spoiled heart.
Staring blankly at the sky I begin to think.
It's a cold night tonight.
The wind pierces my skin as I slowly sulk
towards home.
Why I bother I don't know.
I guess I try too hard, or maybe not enough
Don't hear my laugh or see my smile.
I stare at the blank road ahead; waiting for a sign
of life.
There is none.....
Maybe I'm dead?
I shake that dreaded feeling away.
There, I see the light of my house: warm and
comforting.
I grasp the handle as I fall to my knees.
What's happening?
As I sink into a deep sleep I remember.
I was stabbed.
Pierced through my heart by wretched words
Hate and madness swims through my head as I
take my last breaths.
Forever I will be lost.
Forever wandering that long, lonely street.

Help

sitting here crying in the dark
trying to mend my broken heart
nothing can fix this mess
can't take anymore stress
need somebody close
help fight the demons and ghosts
forever haunting me
breaking who I used to be
I keep dying inside
yes I have lost my mind
am I even worth saving?
because my whole world is just caving
I can't take anymore
here I'll lie across floor
darkness consuming my soul
my body is taking a toll

Desperate

I've been wrong all along
What I inspire you desire
One last chance, at our romance
We need to try, you and I
Issues came to light, I don't want to fight!!
I hear you now, and I wonder how
Please change your mind, you will find
How I can be, you will see
Change your heart, don't depart!
I know you care, I would not dare
To push you away, please just stay
I will pretend, it's not the end
I try to be brave, but then I cave
I hope and pray each and every day
That you come back, we get on track
With the life we seek, sorry I am weak
Without you here, I have lots of fears
Of being alone, I'll wait by the phone
For you to call, I want you all
Never again, you are my friend
A man so dear, please come near!!!
And hold me tight, all through the night
Wipe my eyes, hear my cries
Honest and true, I belong to you
Prayers and hope, I try to cope

If we don't try then I will cry
Feelings so deep, I try to keep
My head held high, and wonder why
For what I've done, I want for none
Forever it's you, and I will stay true

You

I wanted to be your world, but I have failed.
bridges were burned, and the ship has sailed
Away from me, as far away as you can
you've had enough, done being my man.
We are both hurt, stubborn and naïve
who would imagine, that we would now grieve
The loss of our friendship, as husband and wife
my heart is so broken, I don't want this life
Invisible hurt, trust issues, dismay
never thought our life, could end up this way
Promises broken, second chances run dry
I can only look back, and wonder why?
Try as I might, I can't change your mind
your heart it has broken, you refuse to find
A way back in, to try once more
my eyes fill with tears, as you walk out the door
I fall to my knees, my mind fills with dread
I wish there was more, but I've broken that
thread
You held on for so long, with hope in your heart
always remained, never looking to depart
But words have been said, and try as I might
I now face the truth, as you walk out of sight
Till death do us part, a promise we made
broken, alone, I'm feeling betrayed

Hope remains, to you I stay true
all wounds heal, we can start anew
Try we must, use this learning curve
to be together, just what we deserve.